TO: Jo

Best

Michael Black 1998

MW00614640

The World's Greatest Sharpshooter:
Keeping History Alive

By: Michael Blackburn

The World's Greatest Sharpshooter: Keeping History Alive

Copyright 1998, Accolade Promotions

All rights reserved. No part of this book may be reproduced in any form or by any means without prior written permission from the author except for brief quotations embodied in critical essay, article, or review. These articles or reviews must state the correct title and author of this book by name.

Library of Congress Cataloging in Publication

Published by:
Arrowhead Classics Publishers
P.O. Box 4189
Sevierville, TN 37864

Cover Design: Richard Long

ISBN No. 1-885640-36-6

.

DEDICATION

Dedicated to Dana, my wonderful wife and Amy, my precious daughter. This is the most important page in this book. It's my opportunity to tell my two best friends thank you and I love you both. If I ever have to make a choice between the two of you and my career, I'd throw the guns off the mountain.

World's Greatest Sharpshooter

Table of Contents

FORWARD

Michael Blackburn is a living picture of history. Even in this day and age, he remains compassionate, honest, and confident enough to open his heart to the world. This book is a result of Michael's drive to keep a special piece of the past alive in the hearts and minds of Americans. Although he has exceeded the records set by Annie Oakley and Buffalo Bill Cody, these two are Michael's heroes and have been his inspiration through the years. They paved the way for Blackburn's own career.

For a man who is known world-wide as the World's Greatest Sharpshooter, Michael's humility is astounding. When asked about his ability in marksmanship, he will give credit first to the almighty (Yahúweh), then to years of practice. Michael calls his talent ' a gift'. He rarely misses a shot while performing. Sharp shooting, as well as showmanship have become second nature to him.

In this book you will read about a gifted, remarkable boy who grew up to be the World's greatest shot. It is an exciting and unique book at a rare talent, and his journey toward his dream. Truly, this story will have a familiar ring to any reader because there is heartache, elation, disaster, and triumph. But above all, there is hope.

Chapter One

"Eagle Eye"

Michael Blackburn was born in Salem, Illinois on July 29th, 1950. His parents, Bob and Pat, also have a daughter Barri and another son, Patrick. The family actually lived in Kinmundy, Illinois, a small town having a population of only 800. He has many fond memories of his early years in this small rural village. One such memory dates back to the birth of his younger brother. That day, a "plus one" was painted on the town sign. He attended grammar school there and he remembers that his father was a member of the city council.

Michael loved to watch Western movies on television

1

and was especially interested in the gun fights. He developed a keen yearning for a gun of his own. He would engage in many such gunfights with his friends, using a stick for a six-shooter. He constantly pestered his father to buy him a bb gun. "You're just to young for a bb gun, son" was the usual answer.

His Great Great Grandfather, Issac Etchason, lived about thirty miles away in the small Illinois town of Flora. Issac, married to a full blooded Cherokee, was quite a character in his own right. In addition to being a deputy sheriff, he was also a well known and respected gunsmith. The Blackburn family would visit often and young Michael spent many weekends with Grandpa Etchinson. The elderly man, as is the case with most grandparents, was asked for many things by the visiting grandchildren. Young Michael, however, wanted a gun and was relentless in his pursuit for one. He saw all the guns that were in his grandfather's shop to be repaired, and he wanted one that would be his very own. The old man had a small area in the house inclosed by a curtain, that was his shop. Michael would spend hours just watching him, and, of course, pestering him for a gun.

One day Grandpa Issac gave in. He got an old rusty Stevens "Crackshot" .22 caliber rifle from a corner of the modest shop. The gun was worn out but would appease the young boy for awhile, it was hoped. Michael watched carefully as his grandpa, in the interest of safety, removed the firing pin. The gun was then given to the grandson to be used as a toy. The old man's mind was put to ease knowing that the gun could not be fired.

A mistake had been made by allowing young Michael to watch when the firing pin had been removed. The boy

2

figured the problem out quickly and went to work. He found a nail about the right size but a little too long. He simply cut it the approximate length of the firing pin and inserted it into the old single shot Stevens. He was familiar with the "junk drawer" in the shop where some old .22 shells awaited. After getting himself a handful of these shells, he was soon behind the chicken house, a spot far enough away so as to keep anyone from hearing the shots. He loaded the old Stevens and let her rip, receiving a burned forehead for his trouble. This was Michael's Blackburn's first important lesson in gun safety and it had been a good one. It has stuck with him throughout his career.

It wasn't too long after the above episode that Bob Blackburn took his son to the local hardware store to purchase a bb gun. It was a shiny new Daisy. A Red Ryder! It was just what the boy had wanted. Arriving back home and receiving the usual admonition from his mother; "You be careful- you'll shoot your eye out", he was shooting. He would shoot all day long, once keeping a squirrel up a pole all day. He relates that his father could whistle like a train and that was his signal to quit shooting and come in for supper.

A supply of ammunition soon became a problem and the boy started doing odd jobs, such as mowing yards, to get the funds to buy more bbs. The word of his shooting prowess soon spread throughout the small community. His friends began to call him the Unbelievable gunman.

His first targets were walnuts, hickory nuts, and any nut that hung from a tree. He hit every target and slowly began to notice that he could see each bb coming out of the barrel and going all the way to the target. He instinctively knew where that bb was going to hit. He also, at this young age, could count the times that a bird flapped it's wings. He could focus his eyes, much like the "zoom" feature on a camera. He decimated the nut crop that year. He also shot a few birds and regrets that to this day.

Shortly after that his grandpa and great uncle Noah Martin took him rabbit hunting. In fact, Grandpa Issac was known to "bag" more rabbits with a pistol than the other men did with shotguns! He was the local hunting sensation until young Michael began to go with them. Michael was now in possession of a family heirloom, a Stevens single shot .410 shotgun. His father, now enthused by the boy's shooting skill, had reblued it and given it to him as a present. Michael remembers those hunts well. His Uncle Noah had two beagle dogs named "Bead" and "Lead", they were so named because a shooter first had to draw a bead and then lead a running rabbit if you wanted to hit him. The older men would flush rabbits just to see if the boy could hit them. There was a lot of rabbit stew on the supper table in those days, since all game was eaten. Michael will tell you today; "If you're not going to eat it - don't shoot it!"

Those days in Illinois were fun days- growing up days. His nick-name "Eagle Eye" was widely known and he was a hero of sorts to the other kids. He was now working several odd jobs and spending all his money on ammunition, .410 shotgun shells as well as bbs.

One of these jobs was mowing grass for Mr. Deke Ingrams. Mr. Ingrams owned the local grain elevators and had taken a liking to the boy. Michael's mother worked for Ingrams as a bookkeeper. One day, Mr. Ingrams heard that Michael's father, due to his position on the city council, had been invited to a duck shoot at a local hunting preserve.

Seeing the young man outside mowing, Ingrams approached him and said "I've got a couple of shotguns inside, why don't you go see if you like one of them." Michael went inside and sure enough, there they were, behind the door, just as Mr. Ingram had said. He chose the less fancy gun, and brought it outside, saying; "Mr. Ingram, can I borrow this one?" The reply was swift, "No, boy you can't borrow it, you can have it, it's yours!" The boy couldn't believe his good fortune. It was a brand new Remington Model 870, 20 gauge pump shotgun. The "Eagle Eye", now 13 years old, would bag many ducks at the Rodale Acres Hunting Preserve with this wonderful thoughtful gift.

Those boyhood days, in Illinois, would soon come to an end. The Blackburn family, with the young marksman in tow, moved to Hill City, Kansas

World's Greatest Sharpshooter

Pat   Barry   Michael
Patrick   Bo

Michael At Age 4.

Michael At Age 16.

Chapter Two

"Pheasant Country"

The Blackburn Family adjusted quickly to their new surroundings in Kansas. Hill City was a small town in the Northwestern part of the state, not far from the Colorado and Nebraska state lines. Unlike Illinois, the new area was a flat plain with seemingly endless fields of planted crops. Even though small and sparsely populated, it was well known for one thing- pheasant hunting.

In early winter, right after all the crops had been harvested, pheasant season would open. The small town would welcome hunters from all across the country and would be hard-pressed to accommodate them all. There were only two small restaurants in Hill City so several churches came to the rescue. Long before daybreak, breakfast would be cheerfully served by these congregations to hungry hunters from all over.

Pheasant hunting was a big deal for the little town. Some of the local taverns would offer a free drink to the man who brought in the longest tail feather as a part of the community effort to make the annual guests feel welcome. The fields were filled with hunters and the hunting was good.

Michael Blackburn, now a teenager attending high school, liked Kansas. He had made many friends and his shooting prowess was well known. During pheasant season he saw to it that the family had plenty of wild game to eat. Michael still says that his mother could prepare pheasant better than anyone.

Michael secured a job cleaning up used cars for the local Chevrolet/Oldsmobile Dealer. The dealership was owned by the Money family and the job provided funds to buy ammunition. The job required him to be at the dealership after school and on Saturdays so most of his shooting was done on Sundays. At age 16, using his part-time job as a reference, he bought a 1951 Willy's Jeep. He made the payments on time and soon had established a good credit record.

Now, with the added responsibility of a payment, he accepted a Sunday job. He was contracted by a local rancher to poison prairie dogs. These small, determined animals would create havoc on ranches in the area. They would actually build "cities", a labyrinth of tunnels and holes covering a large expanse of pasture land. Cattle would step into the holes which resulted in many broken legs. The ranchers had no choice but to fight back. The standard method of doing so was to poison the "critters". This was accomplished by pouring the lethal substance on cow "chips", their favorite food, and then placing them in the holes. Michael performed this duty for a couple of Sundays but another idea had taken root in his mind.

He asked the rancher; "Do you mind if I shoot the prairie dogs?" The man replied; "I don't care how you do it - just get rid of em!" The boy went to the local hardware store and, using his good credit record, bought a new Winchester Model 94 .22 caliber rifle.

He had developed a plan and he had everything that he would need. Well almost everything - one thing was missing and he would soon solve that problem. He found a piece of one inch scrap wood for use as a rest for the barrel of the new rifle. He cut a small valley in one end to accept the rifle barrel and a deep notch in the other end to slide onto the side window of the old Jeep. Sunday came and he drove the old truck right out into the middle of the pasture. He parked so that one of the prairie dog villages was directly away from the passenger side window. He slid the homemade rest onto the window and placed the barrel on the rest. He would crank the window up or down for elevation. It wasn't long before prairie dogs were no longer a problem for the ranchers. Prairie dogs are a nuisance animal and cannot be eaten.

It was during this episode that the young shooter discovered that sights could be adjusted. He had always, when shooting stationary targets, simply compensated for any inaccuracy. If the rifle shot high and to the right, he would simply aim low and to the left. On moving or aerial targets he didn't worry about it. Since he saw the bullet coming out of

9

the barrel and going to the target, he didn't aim anyway. He had been shooting quarters out of the air for quite some time and really didn't think it was a big deal.

He remembers one occasion very vividly. It was the first time that he was called a liar, something that would occur many times during his career. It still occurs today. One evening, while riding in the old Jeep with a buddy, he mentioned that the could hit a quarter in mid-air with a .22 rifle. The other boy quickly responded; "You're a liar," with a smile on his face. That's all it took.. He immediately grabbed the rifle and got out of the truck. By the lights of the old truck he flipped several coins into the air and hit them all. He then asked the boy; "Am I a liar?." Now it was Michael's turn to smile.

After graduation from high school he entered Hutchinson Junior College. While there, for only one semester, his priorities began to change. He was now thinking more about girls and a job than about shooting. He wanted more out of life and was soon working in the oil fields. In Kansas, during the late 1960s that's where the money was. He worked on a drilling rig for about a year before becoming disillusioned. This was dangerous work and he had seen many men injured and more than one killed.

The family moved back to Illinois and Michael, now a young adult, tagged along. He would find his place in life back where it all started - Salem, Illinois.

Chapter Three

"Workin on the Railroad"

Now back in Illinois, among family and old friends, Michael was, like most young men, searching for his place in the world. He was still more interested in getting a job than shooting.

He had several relatives that worked for the railroad. It was good steady work and it paid well. He remembered that Grandpa Isaac Etchason had worked for the railroad in the early days of steam engines. His job had been to fill the giant engines with water. He went to the employment office of the Chicago and Eastern Illinois Line to fill out an application. While in the office, one of his cousins, who had worked for the company a few years, saw him. His relative yelled to the employment supervisor; "Hey, give that boy a

11

job---he's my cousin." Michael was given a switch key, a lantern, and an employee guide book and told to report to work that same evening. He had been hired as a brakeman. Later he would be promoted to conductor. In fact he became the youngest conductor on the line.

Even though he had not done a lot of target shooting for a year or so, he had enjoyed hunting. His hunting buddies were amazed at the accuracy exhibited by their friend. They spread the word, especially throughout the C&EI Line. His income had increased dramatically and he bought guns, a lot of guns. He loved firearms and amassed quite a collection in those days.

He took up target shooting again and was, amazed that his talent was still there. Shooting quarters was still not a big deal for him. He began to take a .22 rifle with him on some of his working trips. As conductor, he would ride in the caboose. He admits, today, that he did a lot of target shooting out of the window of that caboose. It's a good thing that the railroad never discovered that fact!

Now shooting more than ever he needed an ever increasing supply of ammunition. One of the stops on the C&EI Line was Popular Bluff, Missouri and he found a store there where ammo was inexpensive. He recalls hiding the ammo in a large suitcase, and on one occasion, actually breaking the handle off the suitcase while loading it into the caboose. That's a lot of ammo!

Michael had vacationed in Pigeon Forge, Tennessee and had fallen in love with the Smoky Mountains. The small town, nested in the foothills of the "Smokies" near Gatlinburg, was a beautiful place. The folks there seemed to be very friendly and there was plenty of good hunting and a lot of wide open space. Michael bought a cabin in the sleepy East Tennessee town and he would enjoy many hours of solitude there.

Back in Illinois, the shooter was receiving more and more calls to display his talent. One call, however was different. It would tell him the tragic story of a family who had lost all their possessions in a fire. The family home and all it's contents had been destroyed, leaving them with nothing. He knew what he had to do. He would put his amazing gift to work in the form of a benefit. The time and place was arranged and he put on a real show. Targets were exploded everywhere and the crowd loved it. The shooter would name the next shot and audience would pledge money, to be given to the family, if he made the shot successfully. Plenty of money was raised for the family that day.

The calls picked up, he was now performing at county fairs and gun shows. Even thought still working for the railroad, he was starting to make good money, $100.00 to $300.00 per show. He now accepted his talent, although not understanding it, and began to think about a career in shooting. He knew that many others, who possessed great talent, had made it, so, why couldn't he?

He bought a brand new Buick LeSabre and paid it off in just one season with the proceeds from the many bookings that were coming his way. His efforts were working so he decided that he would "reach for the stars."

There was, however, a down-side to this new found success. He was excited about the thought of a career in shooting, but it seemed no one else was. He was hearing statements like "You'll never make it", "It's a pipe dream", and "You're a fool chasing a fool's dream", and "You had better stick with a good job." These comments were coming from friends and, yes, even family members. He really had trouble understanding their attitude. After all, it was his dream. He wanted them to cheer him on, to be proud and happy for him.

He was soon asked to come to the rescue of a small local school. The school was in Racoon Township and Michael's big heart would not allow him to say no. He remembers that he had broken his glasses, and gone to buy a new pair the day before this benefit. He got the glasses, but the optometrist would not accept payment. His big heart had become well known throughout the region. His performance played a large part in saving the school from closure.

Not long, thereafter, he heard of the plight of a small boy who needed a kidney transplant. The boy needed the new kidney to survive and the family was destitute. The shooter was soon in touch and a time and place were agreed upon. This young boy and his situation had really touched Michael. Remembering the earlier benefit for the burned out family, he thought of a new plan. Before, he had called each shot, but this time he would let audience members call the shots. They would tell him what shot to make and then pledge money to be paid in the event that he was successful. Lots of strange shots were asked of him that day and he hit them all. Lots of money was also raised for the boy that day. Some of the shots, called out during that benefit, remain a part of Michael's performances today.

He added a new dimension to his performances, which were many, at about this time. He would become a showman. A keen interest was also developing- an interest in history. Buffalo Bill Cody, and Annie Oakley were two of the greatest shooters of the past that he had heard about. He wanted to know more so he began to study about the lives of the heroes of the Wild West. He discovered some new names, such as Ad Topperwein and Herb Parsons. Buffalo Bill had put together a traveling "Wild West" show and Annie Oakley had been it's star performer. The more Blackburn read, the more he wanted to know and he soon fell in love. He loved the memory of Annie Oakley, "Little Miss Sure Shot", and soon learned that she held several records. She held the record for hitting the smallest target in mid-air with a .22 rifle. She had hit a dime. The one day endurance record was also held by Annie. She had shot at five thousand 3 inch glass balls in one day. She had missed over 200 times. Michael Blackburn would, although not knowing it then, shatter both these records.

He read about Tombstone and it's historical characters. Doc Holiday was his favorite. He, however, continued his love for Annie Oakley and, even today, the mention of her name will put a smile on his face.

The city of Salem, Illinois contacted him about putting his name on the city sign. It would say; "Welcome to Salem - The home of Michael Blackburn." Still receiving a lot of criticism from family and friends, he was awed by this offer of respect for his blossoming career. The sign went up and a marriage was over. Now, with plenty of bookings and a burning desire for greatness, Michael quit the railroad.

15

World's Greatest Sharpshooter

ANNIE OAKLEY - Michael's Hero.

Michael breaks Annie Oakley's record.
6 Hours 30 Minutes.

2" Square Oak Blocks.

16

Chapter Four

"Let the Good Times Roll"

Michael went to his place of solitude, the cabin in Pigeon Forge, Tennessee. He spent some time trying to sort it all out. He had an unbelievable talent, he knew that for sure. But, he also had a dream. In his younger years, he thought that everyone could shoot the way he could but, slowly, the realization had come that he was different, that he just might be the best. What he couldn't understand was the reaction of others. During the time that he was doing free shows, picnics and friendship shoots, everything seemed fine. Everyone had been on his side. It was only when success came his way that it changed. He wondered why all people didn't follow their dreams just like he had. Maybe they had, or at least started, and then been stopped by all the criticism.

"That was it!" The others hadn't been strong enough to make it through all the negativity thrown at them by friends and relatives. He wondered if he could make it through. It had been coming from all directions and it hurt.

He did a lot of shooting, it helped to console him. This was not done for an audience, he did it for himself. He expended a lot of ammunition in those days, he shot all manner of targets with a wide array of guns. He still had that Daisy Red Ryder bb gun, the one that had meant so much to him in his youth, and he shot it for hours every day. He discovered that he could hit a bb in mid-air with a bb from the daisy. This was a feat that he did so much that it became second nature. It would, one day, be a part of his phenomenal rise to greatness.

Michael returned to Illinois and before long the word was out, the sharpshooter was back in town. The phone was ringing again and he couldn't resist. Amid much criticism he, again was dazzling audiences with the most amazing shooting anyone had every seen.

He accepted more and more bookings during this time, one of which he remembers well. It was in Salem, a local, hometown, show. It was an event that he felt important because it would be filmed by a television crew from St. Louis to be aired on NBC. One shot, in particular, had been selected for the crew to film. It was an easy shot for Michael, he had done it many times before. He would toss a 12 gauge shot shell into the air and shoot off the very tip. He would use a 12 gauge shotgun to accomplish this feat. When the tip was shot off, the shot inside would spill out. Audiences loved it! He performed the shot several times for on-lookers and had several shells, with their tips shot off lying around. A local gunsmith was helping the shooter and, while waiting for the film crew to arrive, decided to cut the brass off these shells. Michael would use them during a later performance. Since the primers were still intact, he would toss them into the air and set off the primer by hitting it with a .22 bullet. It was completely safe since the charge had been taken out. One of these rounds was set off by the sawing process and several pieces of glass were embedded in Michael's eyes. After having the pieces removed, luckily there was no permanent damage. The incident, however was a key ingredient in safety becoming "priority one" in all his performances. He was developing a philosophy that would stick with him throughout his career.

Once, in Decatur, Illinois, after an exhibition, a reporter from the Decatur Herald, confronted him. The man was anti-gun and he was letting everyone in the lingering crowd know it. He raved about how guns kill people and that they should be banned, all of them! After a five minute tirade the reporter seemed shocked at the shooter's reply. "I don't think everyone needs to own a firearm but everyone needs to know how to safely handle one. It's the same with guns", the shooter continued."The use of a firearm to entertain folks," he said, "It is an art." The reporter was deeply impressed and wrote that he thought that Michael Blackburn's time had come to do great things for the art of shooting.

In spite of all the criticism, the sharpshooter was accepting bookings. He was scheduled to perform at a large show in Oklahoma and was served with divorce papers the day before leaving. He did the show, knowing that his marriage was over for good. He was now averaging $500.00 per show and, without any agent or promoter, was getting bookings everywhere.

This time it was different, he wasn't down-he was up! He would follow his dream no matter what! He would show them all!

He had read about Herb Parsons, one of the all time great sharpshooters. Herb had passed away but this modern shooter respected his prowess immensely. Herb Parsons had been known as the "Winchester Exhibition Shooter" for a number of years before his death. Michael decided, then and there, that he would call the folks at Winchester. "If Herb Parsons can do it, I can do it", he thought. After some research, he discovered that he must direct the call to U.S. Repeating Arms Company in New Haven, Connecticut. He called and called and called, being transferred to a different person each time. Finally, he got through to Charlie Rhodes, the company's vice president of marketing. He told Mr. Rhodes about some of the shots that he could do and all of the shows that he had done. Charlie Rhodes, like everyone else who had never witnessed such shooting, simply could not believe what he was hearing. He asked for some form of documentation, suggesting newspaper clippings and video footage. Michael had some newspaper clippings but he did not have a video. Not to be beaten, he told Mr. Rhodes, "I'll make a video."

He went to a nearby rental store and rented a video camera and tripod. There was a small field near home and that site was selected. He had practiced shooting there many times. The tripod was set up although not very well, and the camera was attached. The sharpshooter looked through the camera in order to determine where he should stand to do the shooting. He was alone in this venture or so he thought. The old black hound dog that had been a trusted companion wasn't about to change now. Every time the shooter would get positioned and ready to begin, this "friend" would run up and lick his leg. With the camera rolling, he would say; "Get away from here dog." It was a pointless effort since that dog was determined to be a movie star. So Michael started doing some shots. The video was made with tilted camera and leg licking dog very much evident.

The video and newspaper clips were mailed to Charlie Rhodes and, even though the video was crude and amusing, the awesome talent was evident. Michael Blackburn was invited to the company headquarters in New Haven, Connecticut for a meeting. Mr. Rhodes picked the shooter up at the airport and drove him to a hotel. Mr. Pelton, the company's owner would meet him there the next morning. Pelton and Rhodes arrived on time and after breakfast the three men drove to the sprawling complex that was U.S. Repeating Arms, Inc. He was there, it was hard to believe because Winchester Arms had been around for a long time, and their name was respected by shooters everywhere.

Upon entering the main building, he was immediately impressed. There, in the foyer, was a statue of John Wayne. That's right, there was "The Duke", as big as life, and he was holding a Winchester rifle. He was taken on a tour of the plant and introduced to many of the workers and invited to take a look at some guns in a back room. These guns were not for public viewing he was told. In fact, some were illegal. There were guns in that room that the young shooter had never heard of before. Among others, he saw a "cracker box shotgun and a fully automatic, belt fed, 12 gauge. Michael was in his element, around guns and people who loved guns and he was getting some respect also.

The next stop would be the board room. The young shooter was allowed to sit in the chairman's seat and it was explained to him that this was where all the important decisions were made. Mr. Pelton, the owner said; "Mr. Blackburn, I would like to see what you can do". An exhibition shoot had been arranged for the following day. Michael agreed to do the performance. It would take place at the Laymen Shooting Range and, of course, only Winchester guns would be used.

The performance was no different than any other and the Winchester "Brass" was impressed. None of them had ever seen shooting like what they saw that day. Targets were flying everywhere and, in rapid succession, all were hit. It was the rifle shooting that really astounded the executives because some of them, at least, were almost impossible to believe, even after seeing them done. One example was the shooting of grapes in mid-air with a .22 caliber rifle. Any shooter might get lucky and hit one, but this shooter was hitting them all.

Michael Blackburn gained a new title that day. He would become the "Winchester Exhibition Shooter, the first since Herb Parsons. He was on a roll, his career had risen to heights that, only a few years ago, he would not have believed possible. He had also gained a new friend, Charlie Rhodes.

His fame was spreading and he was, with the help of U.S. Repeating Arms, getting bookings far and wide. He had put it all together himself. No managers, agents, or promoters had ever been in the picture. Since he was doing so well on his own, he figured that, with a promoter, things would be even better, maybe a lot better. He had heard that all the "big names" had agents and promoters, so why not him. "That's it, I'll find a promoter", he said to himself.

He decided to take his time in finding a promoter. He wanted the right one, not just anybody, but one that would and could get the job done. After all, he was already flying pretty high. His shooting prowess was widely known and he was having fun, traveling, and dazzling crowds at county fairs and other events throughout a wide area.

He had performed at an event called "Prairie-esta" in Russell, Kansas, the home of Senator, and later presidential hopeful, Bob Dole. He was there for three days, doing shows each day, and was given the use of a limousine. Even though a meeting with Senator Dole was not in the cards, he was treated like royalty. He also met a local business man who impressed him very much. The man's name was Bill Hickert and Michael still speaks fondly of him today.

He traveled to Saint Joseph, Missouri for an especially large event. It was the "God and Country Rally", one of the shooter's favorite events. His show, now containing a lot of showmanship and spiced up with "down home" humor, was well received. Having made sure that the guns were unloaded and secure, he was signing the first autographs when he, out of the corner of his eye, noticed an elderly gentleman making his way through the crowd. The man was the local bee keeper and as he approached, he yelled; "Son, Can you hit a bumblebee?" The sharpshooter answered; "If you can catch one, I can shoot it!" This exchange was done to the delight of the large audience still gathered at the site. The beekeeper had noticed a nest close by and quickly had a bumblebee in a red bandana. The shooter got into position and, when released the bumblebee flew directly towards the crowd. The bee was smart, no shot was taken. Another bee was soon captured and released. This bumblebee should have followed his friend's route. He flew away from the crowd and was vaporized by one shot from a Winchester 30-30. Michael then told the crowd how he, once, had shot the feathers off a woodpecker so as to recognize him later. The crowd went wild with laughter.

All these performances and practice shooting was consuming large amounts of ammunition. The shooter called Charlie Rhodes and asked that the ammunition be supplied by Winchester. Rhodes told him that the ammo would have to come from another division of the company, the Olin Corporation. He was told to call Olin and tell them that Mr. Rhodes had said to send him ammo at once. The Olin Company sent the ammunition.

He was flown to Winchester, Virginia at the request of McElroy Metals. He was flown there on the company jet and asked to dress as a "Winchester Rough Rider." He had never heard of such a thing but looking forward to the show. The company CEO drove him to the show site, where he was presented with the "outfit" that he would wear. His assistants told him that he looked rather ridiculous in the garb. He was, however, paid $500.00 for the event and had, again, been treated well. The soft-spoken "country-boy" was riding high. He was still thinking about a promoter, and, even though things were good, believed that the right man could take him to the very top.

Michael Blackburn is a very appreciative person and is extremely loyal to those who help him, especially sponsors. Once, while performing at a National Rifle Association event in Columbia, Missouri, this loyalty was tested. It was the Bianchi Cup and it was a pistol match. The sharpshooter had been hired as entertainment for the event. The manager of the firing range, not knowing the terms under which the booking had been arranged, became irate when he saw Michael bring out rifles and shotguns. Everyone else wanted to see him perform, so the show went on. He shot a quarter out of the air with a .22 rifle and, retrieving it, walked over to the VIP box and presented it to the President of the NRA. The quarter had a neat hole, dead center!

U.S. Repeating Arms also had executives in attendance at that event and, during this performance, a Winchester .22 caliber round mis-fired. The shooter knew that it was a live round but not wanting to embarrass the company, he said to the audience; "This shot might have worked if I had reloaded a live round after the last shot". He was later thanked by the Winchester executives.

Life was good, real good for the sharpshooter. He was gaining national fame. He was also thinking about Annie Oakley and the two shooting records that she was held for many years. He was also still looking for a promoter.

World's Greatest Sharpshooter

Michael with Hollis E. Roberts
Chief of Choctaw Nation of Oklahoma.

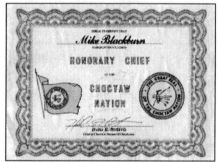

Choctaw Nation Certificate.

Michael practices to be perfect.

Chapter Five

"World Records Shattered"
Part I

Now living in Pigeon Forge, Tennessee, in the place of solitude, and on top of his game, he spent time reading. He wished that he could have met the great sharpshooters of yesteryear, especially "Little Sure Shot." The legacy of these greats had captured his imagination, none more so than Annie Oakley.

She held two world records and they had gone unchallenged for many years. One of these records was for hitting the smallest object, in mid-air with a .22 caliber rifle. Annie had hit a dime and had done so while meeting all qualifications to get the feat recognized by the Guiness Book of World Records. A dime is pretty darn small and, at the time, her feat had been a sensation. It quickly becomes obvious why this record would stand for so long.

World's Greatest Sharpshooter

Michael Blackburn had been hitting bbs in mid-air with a Daisy Red Ryder bb gun for a long time. It really didn't seem like much of a feat to him. He could do it any time that he wished. He knew that hitting the same target with a .22 rifle would be a piece of cake. He would not have a problem with that shot and a grandiose plan began to take shape in his mind. He would break Annie's long standing record.

He drove to the Guiness Museum in Gatlinburg, Tennessee. He paid his way in and inquired about what it took to establish a record in the Guiness Book of World Records. He was quickly told that he would have to contact the international headquarters in London, England. He had no doubt, none whatsoever, that he could pull this one off.

He made the call and quickly discovered that there were some rules, and strict ones at that. The Guiness people did not deal with anything but fact. There would be no room for playing games, this was serious business. The rules were:

1.   The event would have to be witnessed and witnesses had to be credible (judges, law enforcement officers, city father, etc.)
2.   The event would have to be recorded both by still photography and by television news.
3.   The event would have to be publicized by both the print media and by television news.
4.   It would have to be accomplished in a place suitable for the filming. Guiness would not allow any trick photos or video. The background would have to be sky and only sky.
5.   There would only be three attempts allowed. It could not be an all day affair consisting of many attempts and

maybe getting lucky in the process.

The shooter decided to go back in Illinois, to Salem, for this event. He knew a place that would be perfect. It was the Becktell Farm just outside of town. He called the owners and they were elated about the prospect of having such a momentous happening on their farm. It would be done in a large field that met the specification for no obstructions, just clear sky.

A time and date were set and then the work began. Witnesses had to be selected and they must be there at the appointed time. Back ups were contacted, he had to be sure that enough witnesses were on hand. The local county sheriff agreed to serve as did a local mayor. All the local newspapers agreed to send a reporter but television coverage proved to be a greater challenge. After hearing about what the shooter would attempt, they considered it folly. It couldn't be done and sending a film crew would be expensive. After all, they had "real news" to cover. Michael's persistence and excitement, however, won them over and everything was set.

The big day came and everything was in place. Several drop clothes had been laid out on the ground. They were white and reflected a lot of light. A Winchester model 94, lever action .22 caliber rifle was the firearm of choice. Michael tossed up a few bbs so that everyone could focus their cameras as well as their eyes. The television crew could easily be overheard saying; "The whole thing is a waste of time and money, it is impossible for that guy to hit a bb!"

The shooter had heard it so many times before, the negativity, and the doubt. By this time, he had even been called a liar on several occasions. He rejected it, put it out of his mind and remembered that, one time several years ago that he had won ten dollars by shooting a bb out of the air with another bb.

Three bb's were chosen and he held one up to the camera for a close up. It was tiny, a .177 caliber standard bb. One of the observers was heard to comment; "Well, at least you've got three tries." Without any further hesitation, the first bb was tossed and the .22 rifle barked. It had been a hit! "Darn, he actually hit that tiny thing" was heard from the direction of the television crew's position. The shooter, to the amazement of all, responded; "I've got three tries, so I might as well shoot the other two". That's exactly what he did. He hit each of the other two bbs and the entire scene turned to chaos. All of those present wanted to congratulate him, even the television folks!

The action had been captured by slow motion cameras and Michael Blackburn was welcomed into the 1986 edition of the Guiness Book of World Records.

Someone in the crowd yelled; "Son, you are the World's Greatest Sharpshooter!" That was one that he had not heard before but he dismissed it from his mind. He was happy, even elated, but he also felt bad. He wished that he could somehow apologize to Annie. In an instant, less than a second, much less - in the time that it takes to pull a trigger, he had taken this record away from her. He now held it, the world's record for hitting the smallest object in mid-air with a .22 caliber rifle.

During some performances, today, he routinely shoots Rolaids (Micro-skeet) and at a recent event he shot aspirins out of the sky. Within one year the soft spoken "gentleman" shooter would capture Annie Oakley's other record - the one day endurance record.

Chapter Six

"Poor Annie"
Records Shattered, Part II

Since breaking the record for hitting the smallest object and gaining recognition by The Guiness Book of World Records, calls were coming in from everywhere. That event had been well publicized and Michael Blackburn was becoming somewhat famous. He was playing to larger crowds now and loving every minute of it. It had been during the Guiness shoot that a member of the audience had yelled; "Boy, you're the World's Greatest!" This comment, even though appreciated, had, at the time, not been taken too seriously. That had been the first time that he had heard it but, later, he heard it often. He knew that he could duplicate any shot that he ever heard of or read about and was routinely accomplishing shots that no one else had ever done. He had studied the lives of all the great shooters and knew that he could compete with any of them. He wondered if it could be true. Could he be the World's Greatest?

He had asked the local library to order some books. Among them was Annie Oakley's Diary. He thought he knew everything about "Little Sure Shot" but was soon to discover a fact that would greatly disappoint him. Annie, in her diary admitted that she used shot shells in her rifles. She wrote; "I use shot shells in my .22 rifles to make them into exceedingly small bore shotguns in order to hit targets that couldn't possibly be hit with a solid bullet." "Can't possibly be hit with a solid bullet", he asked himself. He had been doing just that since he was seven years old. He had broken one of her records by hitting a bb in mid-air with a solid bullet and was routinely hitting dimes, quarters, aspirin, and grapes with solid bullets. Because of what he had read, he decided to break her other record; the one day endurance shoot. He also decided to do so with solid bullets.

Annie had shot five thousand 3 inch glass balls in one day and, even though missing 228 times, established a record that would stand for a very long time. There is no known evidence to suggest that anyone knew, during her career, that she used shot shells.

Michael wanted to use 2 inch glass balls but none could be located on the open market. Since having them custom made would be too expensive he decided to use charcoal briquets for targets. Two local teenage boys were recruited to keep the guns loaded for a trial run. The shooter bought six large bags of charcoal and a 55 gallon drum was set up in a plowed field near town. The plan was to pour one bag of briquettes at a time onto the top of the drum while keeping the two Winchester .22's loaded. He started shooting and was soon out of charcoal. He would stop shooting only for the time required to make the short trip to town to replenish the supply. He bought all the charcoal on hand at all the stores that day. One clerk, seeing the dust all over him asked; "Are you shooting that charcoal or wearing it?" He shot over 6000 charcoal briquettes in that one day, missing none. He was ready to break Annie's other record. He knew that he could do it.

He would do it, however, with some other type of targets - charcoal was just too dirty. After some thought, wooden blocks were selected. A local sawmill agreed to donate the lumber, 2 inch by 2 inch Oak in long sections. The boards would have to be cut into 2 inch lengths to make the appropriate targets. The owner of a local gun shop, a man that knew the shooter well, had an old John Deere tractor that was equipped with a cut-off saw and he offered it to the shooter. Even though old, it would do the job. The lumber was picked up and a jig was made so that the targets would all be the same. A local Chevrolet dealer offered the use of a new pick-up to be used to transport the targets to the site where the feat would be attempted.

The fairgrounds in DuQuoin, Illinois had been selected as the location for the record breaking attempt. It was more than adequate with plenty of open space, a grandstand with seating for the spectators, and it was near his home town of Salem. Credible witnesses would have to be on hand since this was a challenge to a world record. The local mayor, Mr. Ferguson, and an official from the National Rifle Association had been selected. Seven assistants had also been chosen to keep a supply of targets within the shooter's reach and to keep the eleven Winchester model 94, lever action .22 caliber rifles loaded. Winchester provided the rifles and ammunition.

With everything in order, Michael picked the truck up from the dealer and drove to the place where the targets had been cut. He had not counted the wooden blocks but merely assumed that a truck load would be at least five thousand of them. The truck was loaded to capacity and driven to the fairgrounds.

He was absolutely certain that he could accomplish this feat and take Annie's remaining record from her. After all, he had already shot the six thousand charcoal briquets, without a single miss. Also he had fired the last one hundred or so shots after dark. He had been able to see the targets in the air above the horizon, but not the sights. He really didn't need the sights but he had caught fireflies and smashed them on the sights to orient the barrel. This would be a piece of cake, no different than the previous record attempt.

A large crowd had gathered, the witnesses were in their seats, and the press was on hand to document the shoot. With a huge pile of targets and eleven fully loaded rifles, he started shooting. It was a dreary day with drizzling rain. Many of the people in attendance had suggested that he postpone the effort. He had performed in all kinds of weather at events all across the country and would not be stopped by the rain. A target would be tossed and he would shoot, over and over again, and a rhythm was quickly established. As each target was hit it was retrieved by an assistant and passed to the official observers for inspection. This was a laborious task for all involved and the judges were soon asking for a break. A pile of broken targets were being accumulating in the judges' area and empty shell casings littered the ground. The shooter was hitting them all. Rifles were being loaded quickly from the many boxes of ammunition that had been stacked on folding tables. When one rifle's load had been expended, another fully loaded one was ready. The shooter had opted for eleven rifles to allow time for the barrels to cool. During the practice "charcoal shoot", one of them had become so hot that it jammed. Someone called out "one thousand", then "two thousand". Comments such as "He'll never do it" and "He'll give out if he doesn't take a break" could also be heard.

Finally at the insistence of the officials, a short break was taken. At this time it was noticed that the pile of targets were almost gone. "Surely a pick-up truck will hold 5000 two inch blocks" the shooter said, but it was obvious that the assumption had been incorrect. In fact, the truck load of targets had numbered only about 2500, half the number needed. This situation, however proved to be no problem at all as Michael simply stated; "Just throw the pieces from the other pile." He started shooting again and was hitting pieces of original two inch blocks, ones that had already been torn apart by previous hits. Oak wood splits easily, and when hit by the hyper-velocity rounds, they did so readily.

That day, in the rain and under watchful eyes of official observers, he fired at 5004 wooden targets in six and one half hours, missing only three times. That is a shot every four and one half seconds. He attributes the three misses, a fact that bothers him to this day, to one rifle. One of the guns used that day had the trigger pull altered for exhibition shooting. He shot with his toes during some shows using that rifle which had a trigger pull of only two and one half pounds.

Annie Oakley's other record now belonged to the soft-spoken, down-to-earth country boy and the world would soon know it. The Associated Press had covered the momentous event and the news was being aired all over the world. Annie Oakley had held these records for many years and they, since belonging to Michael, have gone unchallenged. They will be hard to beat. Michael Blackburn could, easily, break them again. At the fairgrounds in Illinois, after breaking the record he shot another 250 pieces of targets one handed again using crushed fireflies on the sights. He hit them all!

Since Annie Oakley's one day endurance record had not been recognized by Guiness, Michael had not contacted them. The breaking of this record, however, was well documented by the media and by credible witnesses. He was now beginning to believe what others had thought for a long time. He was, in fact, THE WORLD'S GREATEST EXHIBITION SHARPSHOOTER!!!!

Chapter Seven

MISTER "M"

With his most recent and successful record attempt now simply a fact the phone began ringing constantly. Michael was on top of his game. He was earning not only respect for his talent but also a very good living. The world-wide press coverage of the one day endurance shoot had a positive effect on his career. He was still the "Winchester Exhibition Shooter", a title he took seriously and with great pride. He was on the road constantly, performing for large crowds at all manner of festivals and county fairs all over the country. His big heart, still very much intact, was drawing him to do benefits in many places and he visited quite a few Children's Hospitals during this period.

He had never had a promoter, but really wanted one

now. He figured that if he could do as well as he was doing working alone, a promoter could really take him to the top. He reasoned, all the "Big Names" had agents and promoters. He began to look, in earnest, for the right person to handle his blossoming career. In reality, this laid-back and trusting sharpshooter was about to enter an arena that he would never, in his wildest imagination, have thought existed.

He secured a booking, on his own, to perform at a festival in a very small town near Bloomington, Illinois. Upon arrival, he was struck by just how small this town really was. There was evidence of a few businesses, now only boarded up storefronts, and not much else. In fact, the only business in operation was the Post Office. There were some houses, the tiny post office, and a town sign-that was it. When the time came for the event to open, he was absolutely amazed at the number of people that crowded into that small town. It was a well promoted event, and he was treated like a king. He was driven around in a beautiful horse drawn carriage all day and picked up in a limousine that evening. The limo would take him to a nice restaurant in a nearby town for dinner. Upon arriving at the restaurant and being seated at the head table he noticed that every table had a complimentary book of matches for the guests. The match books had his name emblazoned on their covers. That was absolutely the neatest and most professional thing that had ever happened at any event that he had ever attended. He was impressed.

His performance had gone well and he estimated the crowd to number around ten thousand people. Later, back home in Salem, he told some friends about the experience. During this conversation there was general agreement that the promotor of that event must be really good. To attract so many people to such a small town had really taken some effort. Someone suggested that Michael should find out who the promotor was and see if he could hook up with him. Michael's career was really going well but he was sure that this person could make things go even better.

Michael knew the folks who had promoted the successful event and contacted them and a meeting was arranged. Actually the event had been promoted by two people, a married couple, who were wealthy farmers in the area. The meeting proved to be exciting with ideas flying all around and they were big ideas too. They would get him more work than he ever dreamed possible, he would be a star. The couple offered him a five year contract with them receiving twenty five percent of all booking fees. Excited and looking toward a bright future, he signed the contract. He seemed to be headed for the "big time".

His phone continued to ring and he would give the information to the promoters who would, in turn, make the deal. He soon began to wonder why their phone wasn't ringing, why all the bookings were from his previous engagements. In fact, over a two year period, the couple did not secure a single booking for him on their own. They simply took a twenty five percent commission on shows that he would have done anyway. There was, however, one instance that they did, in a way, become involved in a booking.

While performing at a trade show that he had attended many times before, Michael met an exhibitor from Milwaukee, Wisconsin who was awed by his amazing talent. The man told the sharpshooter that he was well connected in Wisconsin and thought he could get him work there. Busy with performances and meeting other people at the show, he put the man's comments out of this mind. He had heard it many times before and he knew that if the guy was serious, he would receive a phone call.

One day after the show, and now back in Salem, his phone did ring. The man who called introduced himself as Mr. "M" (not his real name) from Milwaukee, Wisconsin. Mr. "M" related that a friend of his had seen Michael's performances at a trade show and was impressed. The man then asked, "How would you like to do 300 shows a year?" How many shows did you say?", the shooter asked in disbelief. "Three hundred or more every year" was the immediate response. "Sounds real good to me" said the shooter, "When do you want me to start?" Mr. "M", without any hesitation, said "Get in your car right now and get started!" He gave Michael his phone number and hung up. The shooter immediately called his agents.

Even though both the husband and wife had been involved as his agents in the beginning, the wife had actually assumed the role. Michael told her about the phone call and related it had happened too fast and he thought they should ignore the offer. "Oh no" she said, "This could be the break that you've been waiting for. You should go and I'll go with you", she said. He packed his bags and drove immediately to Bloomington where she lived. When he got there she was packed and ready. She was excited about the deal and while raving about the possibilities exclaimed, "Get in my car, I'll drive!"

The two were on their way to Milwaukee and their spirits were high. Three hundred shows a year would compute to big money and the lady agent had convinced the sharpshooter of the possibility. She had called Mr. "M" before leaving, introducing herself and obtaining an address so, now, it was just a matter of getting there.

Finally they arrived and both were dazzled by the surroundings. This was not just a house, this was a huge estate. Michael made the comment: "This place is as big as ten barns!" They were met at the door by Mr. "M", a short man in his mid 60's and escorted into the mansion. It was late, around eleven and the owner of such a grand place was meeting them personally, that was something special!

Upon entering the foyer, the shooter immediately noticed a picture of Frank Sinatra that had been autographed. He remembered reading that "Old Blue Eyes" didn't give autographs to anyone and was duly impressed. Mr. "M" was obviously wealthy and very well connected. The next stop was the den, where the young shooter was offered a glass of cognac and told that it costs $500.00 a bottle. Michael didn't normally drink but figured that if it costs that much he had better drink it and did. The walls of the room were lined with autographed pictures of important people. People such as Clint Eastwood, Sylvester Stallone, and John Wayne. Wow, he was in the "big time" now!

Mr. "M" wanted to talk business right away and threw out some mind boggling figures. He told the sharpshooter; "If you stay with me for one year you will have a six figure bank account and be driving any kind of vehicle you want." The man was beginning to lay it all out but was interrupted by the lady agent, who said; "Let's talk business tommorow, I'm tired and need to get some sleep." Mr. "M", did not like the comment but agreed to continue the meeting the following day. He had arranged for rooms at a nearby motel for both of them and they were soon on their way there. They had spent about an hour with the wealthy little man and that had been enough for Michael. He told the lady agent that he didn't like the setup and thought that they should forget the whole deal and go home. She stated, "We're driven this far, let's see what tommorow brings." They drove on to the motel for some rest and would see what the next day would bring.

They arrived at the mansion at the appointed time, were ushered into the private office, and there met Mr. "M". He was ready to do business and immediately started dialing the phone. He was booking fairgrounds and trade centers all across the country. He would simply look up a number, dial it, and order whoever answered to rent him the facility on a certain date. This guy was scary! Michael remembers one phone call in particular, that Mr. "M" made to Cincinnati, Ohio. After booking the facility there Mr. "M" told the other party, "Now, you're in charge of the union down there and I want you to sell 500 advance tickets." This was followed by the statement; "If you don't come through, I'd suggest that you practice swimming with chains and concrete blocks." During that meeting, while the lady agent was out of the room, Mr."M" told the shooter; "Don't worry about her, she's out of the deal."

That evening his agent informed him that she was going back to Illinois. She explained to the young shooter that he would have to stay, that Mr. "M" needed him there in case questions or impromptu exhibitions came up. He asked her not to leave him there without transportation but she assured him that this was the big break that he had been seeking and that everything would turn out okay. She went home.

The following day a limousine was waiting at the motel

to take the shooter back to the estate. He was told to bring all his luggage, guns, etc. with him since he would be staying in the guest quarters at the estate in the future. When he arrived he was again met by Mr. "M" who informed him that his first performance would be at a trade show in Milwaukee. The fairgrounds had been rented and the entire affair would be put on by his host. He was given three one-hundred dollar bills and told he would be paid one-hundred dollars per day from then on. The man who made the arrangements for the show site wanted to see him shoot-NOW, so they were soon on their way. He did some shots and everyone present was amazed and said so. He told Mr. "M" that he would need an assistant in order to do a full exhibition shooting performance at the upcoming event and suggested that his brother Patrick, be hired for the task. Patrick Blackburn was soon on his way from East Tennessee to Milwaukee. The shooter had told his brother, on the phone, that it was a scary deal and that he thought that some of the people might even be mobsters. His brother came anyway and was put up in the guest quarters. Patrick, needing income was given a job of sorts by a man who owned a fish processing plant, the same man that had made the arrangements for the trade show. The first night, after starting the new "job", Patrick had a lot to tell his brother. He related that all the employees at the plant were convicts on some sort of work release program and that some of them were "real bad dudes." The plant processed all kinds of fish, some even smelling rotten, by grinding them up, bones and all, and compressing the meat into small balls. Even though the process was probably sanitary and big name companies bought these fish balls, the subject of this book will not eat this product even today.

The day of the trade show was approaching and booths were being set up at the fairgrounds, however, one thing seemed to be a little odd. Everything belonged to Mr. "M". Semi truck loads of fishing, camping, and sporting equipment were arriving daily to stock the booths and all of it was the property of the producer, even the trucks! The time came and everyone was excited. Attendance was disappointing and Mr. "M" was very unhappy. The only thing people wanted to see was Michael's shooting. He was scheduled to do one performance, but at Mr. "M"'s insistence, shot all day long.

After that show, Mr. "M" told the shooter that he would be going to Las Vegas, Nevada. He would perform there for 180 days and would be paid $2,000.00 per day. His shows would be at odd hours such as 3 a.m. and during the day he would be required to do "other things." Having already been asked to sign several suspicious documents and getting fed up with the surroundings he refused to be a part of it any longer. He and Patrick left Minnesota and Mr. "M" for good.

During the drive home he did a lot of thinking about the relationship that he had with the agent in Bloomington. She had never secured a booking for him on her own in two years and had left him stranded in Milwaukee. He decided to fire her as soon as he got back home. He was fed up with the whole deal.

After getting home and resting he drove to the agents home near Bloomington and was met with excitement. "I've just got to show you something", she said "Let's go into town." He rode with her to the bowling alley. They went inside and she introduced him to HIS bowling team. They were called the "Sharpshooters" and were attired in beautiful embroidered shirts. He had never been told about the team but was expected to pay for everything. He fired the agent and was presented with a bill for over $4,000.00 for the bowling team and leather bound proposal binders. He later learned that the bowling team had never won a game.

His first agent had taken 25% of all his fees for shows that he would have booked, himself, anyway, had left him in Milwaukee, and run up several thousand dollars in debts for him to pay. Having fired them, he thought it was over, but would soon learn that it wasn't. The contract with them had been for five years, a fact which would cost him his relationship with Winchester and keep him from performing for three more years.

Down in spirit, he returned to the place of solitude-the cabin in the Great Smoky Mountains of East Tennessee.

World's Greatest Sharpshooter

Michael poses for publicity pictures.

Michael splits a bullet with knife edge and hits both targets.

Michael shoots just as well with a pistol.

Chapter Eight

"MUSIC CITY"

Pigeon Forge, Tennessee was a peaceful little town, nestled in the foothills of the Great Smoky Mountains near Gatlinburg. Since buying the cabin, it had offered the shooter a place of solace, a place to think, and after recent events in Illinois and Wisconsin that's just what he needed.

At the time, Pigeon Forge had not yet become the tourist mecca that it is today. The area, today with Dollywood and other attractions plays host to several million tourists each year. The Great Smoky Mountains National Park is the most visited park in America and Sevier County is one of the fastest growing counties in the state.

He was trying to figure it all out, the promoter in Bloomington, as far as he was concerned, had taken him for

47

a ride. The time in Wisconsin had been wasted and now he had lost Winchester as a sponsor. The U.S. Repeating Arms company had called to renew the contract as had been the case every year. He had received a lot of bookings because of his association with the giant corporation and now it was all over. During the negotiations to renew the contract the agent in Bloomington had called Winchester demanding 25 percent of everything associated with that contract. Their contract with the shooter had about three years to run and they were going to enforce it. The president of U.S. Repeating Arms offered the shooter the use of their legal department but, in the end, it cost Michael Blackburn the title "Winchester Exhibition Shooter." He decided that if he had to pay them that he would not perform at all until their contract expired.

Even though the awesome talent was still intact he quit shooting and went to work in the building trades. His work was the erection of log homes from pre-cut kits, much like putting together a giant erector set. He liked the work and was soon in charge of a crew. He had made many friends in the area and was soon being asked to perform at backyard barbecues and the like. He did so, without hesitation, to accommodate friends or friends of friends. Sometimes he would be paid $50.00 and on rare occasions even $100/00. Due to these events, the word spread quickly and one day he received a call from an entertainer in Gatlinburg. He knew the man well, considered him to be a friend, and enjoyed occasional visits to his home. On this occasion, however the subject was business. The entertainer wanted him to sign with his own agent and a meeting was arranged. Michael went to the meeting and listed attentively to all the "big talk." He had heard it all before in Illinois and wasn't about to repeat that situation. He refused to sign.

He was happy and making a living. Both he and his wife, Dana were working. People were beginning to pour into the area to settle permanently and many of them wanted a log home so business was good. In spite of it all, however, the dream just wouldn't die, he was still the "World's Greatest Exhibition Sharpshooter."

One evening he got a call from a man that he had never met. The man had heard of his shooting and had a proposition for the shooter. A meeting was arranged and Michael reluctantly attended. The man said that he owned a theme park in Kentucky and wanted to hire him for the upcoming season. He would pay the shooter $100,000.00 plus expenses and he would be required to perform one show daily. Michael was skeptical at first and asked a lot of questions. The man said "If you don't believe me, just look at this" and showed the shooter a plaque. It was a beautiful trophy honoring the man for his kindness and generosity toward employees at the theme park and congratulating his admission into the Amusement Park Hall of Fame. "Maybe this is real", the shooter thought to himself. This man had been honored and had shown him proof of it, he seemed sincere and was winning Michael over. The man had wanted him and Dana to leave for Kentucky the following week and offered him $1500.00 in cash for travel expenses. It would only be a three hour drive and he didn't really need the money so he turned it down. The man quickly said "I want you to have the money and if you don't take it the deal is off." Now totally convinced of the legitimacy of the deal, Michael and Dana had accepted the money and left to make necessary arrangements. The dream had flooded to the front of his mind once more and he was ready to try for stardom. The couple quit their jobs and packed, looking forward to a new adventure. They were going to earn $100,000.00 that summer and were excited about Michael's career getting back on track.

The day before they were to leave the man phoned to tell them that there had been a small delay in plans. He indicated that it would only take a few days to get it resolved and then they could be on their way. The days passed quickly and the phone rang again, another hitch, nothing to worry about, just a few more days. They waited to receive another call of the same nature. Michael called the attraction in Kentucky and discovered that they had never heard of the man. He even spoke with the real owner-no one there knew this man. They had quit their jobs and were angry about the deal. They just couldn't figure it out, after all this man had given them $1500.00 in cash for expenses, not a promise but cold hard cash. Michael drove to the man's home and confronted him. The man began sobbing and asking for forgiveness. He related that he was a habitual liar and couldn't help himself, that he was in a treatment program but it didn't seem to help. It had all been a lie and he had probably had the plaque made himself, but this pathetic man had actually given Michael Blackburn $1500.00 as expense money to travel to an amusement park that he had no affiliation with whatsoever. Michael never saw the man again but considers this to be the most bazaar occurrence of his entire career.

The couple returned to their jobs, more than a little embarrassed by the experience, and were soon back to a routine existence. A daughter, Amy, came into the world and life was good. Even though fairly content, Michael still dreamed of a shooting career. In spite of recent events, he had memories of days when he was at the top, and they were good memories. He had met many wonderful people and made a lot of friends in those days. While driving nails or sawing logs, thoughts of those days would flood his mind. His employer asked him to do a few performances to help promote the business and he gladly did so. During one of these shows his employer shot some video footage which was later used as part of a promotional package for the resort. This was done without Michael's permission and hurt him deeply.

Michael Blackburn possesses a unique and awesome talent but also is a very sensitive and caring individual. He is trusting, perhaps too trusting, and is a gentleman in every sense of the word. He is somewhat like the coins that he blasts out of the sky-two sided. When performing he is dead serious, almost sinister, and in total control of his space. At other times he is so mild mannered, so respectful of others, and so selfless that an unknowing person would not have a clue about his claim to fame. A big "giver" himself, he is easy prey for the "takers" of the world. This writer, although not there at the time, is sure that he called his first agent "ma'am" while firing her. There would be more disappointment to come.

The couple, still working in Tennessee took a long overdue vacation to Florida. They would attend an event called "Super Ride" in the central part of the state and meet an individual who had heard of the shooter's talent. Even though not performing much, he was still the "World's Greatest Sharpshooter" and was well known throughout the country.

This man was a promoter in the area and had big ideas. He would offer the sharpshooter $500.00 per week to do public relations work for his company and a few promotional exhibition shoots. Dana Blackburn would be employed in an administrative position with the same company. A new and very expensive motorhome was provided for the couple to use during PR trips. It would also serve as a home away from home. They liked Florida and decided to give it a try. The money would be good and Michael could do some exhibition shooting. He was still following his life long dream.

He appeared on talk shows and held press conferences to publicize various events produced by his employer. He did a few shooting exhibitions and, during one, met Cowboy Bobbie Denton, a unique individual, and a person that the shooter liked very much. Several weeks had gone by and there had been no money paid to the couple. Every time the promoter was asked about money he would reply; "Don't worry about it, just stick with me and it will all work out." This would usually be followed by a twenty dollar bill and the admonition, "This should get you by until you get paid." They finally got tired of the promises and demanded their money. They were given $150.00 for expenses and left Florida to return to Tennessee. The "big talker" owed Michael over $6,000.00, a sum that has never been paid.

Back at home in Tennessee, Michael was soon building log homes again. Several years ago, in the 1980's Michael had met William Lee Golden, one of the Oak Ridge Boys. They were in concert in Illinois and had invited the shooter to the performance. Golden was so engrossed in their conversation backstage that he had to be pushed on stage for the show. The music had already started. During this time, Michael had done a show on TNN with Golden, Charlie Pride, and Paul Overstreet. He liked some of the stars that he had met and wondered if maybe his talent would fit. He called Golden to discuss the possibilities and, with the singer's help, secured a booking in Nashville. The dream flooded his head once more, he was going to "Music City", the town where stars were born. "I'll make it big this time" he thought, "I'll be discovered." He had some bad experiences with promoters but he figured that big promoters, Nashville people, would be different. After all, the stars all had agents and they were doing fine.

He was booked to perform at the annual "Jessie James Festival", a large and prestigious event and he was prepared to put on the show of his life. He would show them some real showmanship! He did just that, dazzling the audience with his shooting skill. Right after the show, he was introduced to many people. One of whom was Joe Hupp. Mr. Hupp had a well deserved reputation in the music business. He had created and enhanced many careers over the years. During the conversation it became obvious to the shooter that Mr. Hupp was honest and straight forward. This was true enough, but the crafty promoter could not figure how a person with Michael's talent could be promoted and he told him so. "You've got a novelty act, son - I'm in the music business, I can't help you." Even though this is not what the shooter had expected to hear, he knew that he had talked to an honest man. Wanting to help, Mr. Hupp drove Michael to Opryland, the huge theme park just outside of Nashville to meet Merle Haggard who was scheduled for a performance. After the show he was introduced to Haggard and was invited to accompany the singer to his tour bus. On the way to the bus, in the parking lot, Haggard clashed with some Opryland executives. "I thought I would be staying at the Opryland

Grand Hotel, not the Motel Six", said the singer, "I even had to buy my own breakfast" he added. Laughing, Merle Haggard turned to Michael and said, "You have to jack these big shots up once in a while to keep them straight." The two men spent the evening talking. Michael liked Merle Haggard.

He had met another well known agent by the name of George Mallard. This man also had a good reputation and was called a "starmaker." He explained to the shooter that he only handled singing talent and commented, "What can be done for the "World's Greatest Sharpshooter?" The man wanted to help, however and introduced the shooter to Tony Stampley, the son of Joe Stampley, who had written many songs for Hank Williams. During this meeting a suggestion was made that the three men attend an upcoming private party for Travis Tritt. The shooter was given the time and place and was assured that the other two men would meet him there. The event was held at the posh "Stockyards" and the parking lot was filled with fancy cars. Michael, driving a 1961 Ford pick-up truck, pulled in between two Mercedes automobiles and parked. As promised, the two men were there to meet him and all three entered the establishment. The place was filled with celebrities and the shooter was heady with excitement, "Surely, someone here can help me get to the top" he thought. He was keeping good company that night because the place was teeming with stars. Reba McIntire, The Kentucky Headhunters, Doug Kershaw, Alan Jackson and many other big names were in attendance. Michael had come to the affair all decked out in western attire. It was an event for a country star attended by country stars and he wanted to fit in. Even though he saw only one other person in a cowboy hat, he enjoyed the event very much. His mind was reeling with thoughts of greatness, of fame and respect for his talent. He believed that he could "make it" if he could just stay in Nashville long enough.

Guns were his first love so he got a job in a local gun shop. He liked the work and sold a lot of guns to the stars. He and William Lee Golden continued their friendship and he visited the singer's home on several occasions. Golden owns an old plantation house in a town near Nashville, a place that he shooter fell in love with on his first visit. Golden shared a tenet with Blackburn and it has stuck with the shooter. It has meaning for him and has helped him through some tough times. It is "Man only faces opposition as he advances." He sees William Lee Golden not as a star but as a friend. This friendship continues today.

He was contacted by Merle Kilgore, manager for Hank Williams, Jr. and asked if he would like to meet the star. Having heard about the singer's love of firearms, he said, "Sure." There was a concert coming up at the Thompson Bowling Arena in Knoxville, Tennessee and that is where the meeting would take place. The thought of meeting Hank Williams, Jr. was exciting and being asked to do so made it even better. Williams was an avid hunter and shooter himself and Michael appreciated the star's respect for his talent. The big night came and he and Dana loaded up in the old pick-up and made the drive to Knoxville. The old truck didn't look very good but was fairly reliable, having made the trip to Nashville many times. He had been advised by Kilgore to park near the busses at a certain time and he arrived with time to spare. Security guards were all over the old truck before he and Dana could get the doors open telling them that they could not park there. Michael explained the situation, telling them who he was and that he had been invited. He was allowed to park. While waiting, they met the singing group Diamond Rio and talked with them for quite some time. They were invited to have a snack with the band and enjoyed their company. He considered them to be fine people, all of them. Finally, amid much ballyhoo, Hank Jr. did appear, sauntering past the Blackburns. He did utter a sarcastic "Nice to meet you" as he went by and the couple soon realized what a pointless trip that it had been. He was told that the Diamond Rio group had not been permitted in the area of the Williams' tour bus either. He fondly remembers his short time with the Diamond Rio group. He doesn't have much to say bout Hank Williams, Jr.

At this juncture, you might think that the time spent in "Music City" had been all for naught. If so, you are wrong! Michael Blackburn, "The World's Greatest Exhibition Sharpshooter" was, in fact discovered while in Nashville. He had reached for the stars and he had made it, or so he thought. This episode merits it's own chapter.

"If you reach for the stars, you might get a few blisters along the way."

---Glen W. Turner

CHAPTER NINE

ESPN

Michael, having been in Nashville, Tennessee for sometime and having met several stars in the music business, was well aware that a lot of money could be made on television. He knew that he had the talent and he knew that people from all walks of life had enjoyed his shooting performances. What he needed was to meet the right person, someone who had connections in the industry and who would recognize the marketability of his talent. He was looking for the proverbial "break".

The shooter was approached by a man at the conclusion of an exhibition performance at a festival near Nashville. It was the "Jessie James Re-enactment" festival and the show had gone well. The gentleman introduced himself as Jim Sowards, a television producer and marketing specialist. Jim was involved with the production of "The Jessie James Gang Re-enactment" which was to be aired on an up-coming segment of "The Ralph Emery Show." After congratulating Michael on his performance, Sowards invited him to appear on television for an interview. Michael was elated, "This is it - this is going to be the break that I've been waiting for", he thought to himself.

With the dream of fame and fortune again flooding his mind, he agreed to the interview and a time and date was set. The time came and the shooter arrived early and was full of excitement. As a result of the interview, he was told that another meeting had been requested by another production company. There had been a very positive response from viewers and he was told "The Big Brass like you, boy!"

Meetings were held, "big" meetings with "big" people, and an idea was hatched for a new segment, a segment in which he would star. He was involved in the planning and his input was respected. The segment would be called, "The American Shooter". Many questions remained unanswered such as, who would sponsor the show, who would host it, etc., but it would be producted, that decision had been made. Michael knew, at that point, that he had "made it". He would be on national television and the monetary figures that were being thrown at him were mind boggling. "You'll get forty percent of all the sponsor money." "You'll have residuals on re-runs." "You can sell videos." and "You'll be rich" were some of the comments that he was hearing. He knew that these comments would bring him tens of thousands of dollars when the footage was sold to television.

Many meetings were held and some of the questions began to have answers. Michael wanted Chuck Conners, who starred in the popular series "The Rifleman", to host the show. As a boy, he watched with awe as Conners, portraying the role of Lucas McCain, fired the special short barreled .44 Caliber Rifle on the show. The "brass" agreed and Conners was contacted. The famous actor agreed to host the show and was put under contract. One evening, heavy with excitement and at home, Michael's phone rang. It was Chuck Conners calling to say that he was looking forward to working with "The World's Greatest Sharpshooter". The filming was due to take place soon and the two would meet in person.

This was almost enough to make the country boy shooter's heart stop. He was actually going to meet Chuck Conners. This, coupled with all the money, the fame, and the respect for his talent would make up for all those road weary years. He was about to see the payoff, FINALLY! Conners and Blackburn would talk frequently during the next few weeks, mostly about guns.

Sadly, Chuck Conners passed away just before time to film the first thirteen segments of "American Shooter". It was a blow to Michael but he knew that he would have to press on with the show. The filming was done and enough footage was captured to air many segments. The shooter filmed many of the shots that he normally performs and, since he rarely misses, the filming was completed in a few days. He was paid $2400.00 for this effort but he knew that the big payoff would soon come his way.

The executive producer exclaimed; "This is good stuff, we won't have any trouble selling it". It didn't take long to sell it and the rest is history. It would be aired on ESPN and would be seen by an international audience. Michael has heard that the show was seen in sixty countries over a two year run.

The "American Shooter" show was nominated for an

EMMY in the "Most Dramatic" category and Michael was told that his segment received 87% of the show's fan mail. He was told that the show drew a rating of 1.2, a number that he didn't understand the significance of for quite sometime. It is, in fact, a good rating. The show was soon being sponsored by industry heavyweights like Leupold Stevens and The Times - Mirror Company. The "Shot of the Week" segment starring Michael Blackburn, The "World's Greatest Sharpshooter" would run and re-run for four years and then be re-run again on vigettes titled: "Amazing Shots". The footage still, today, can be seen on ESPN I and ESPN II and on TNN as well.

The soft-spoken, country boy shooter - the star of the segments, the talent behind the fan mail and ratings was never paid one red cent of the promised percentages. His total compensation for the entire experience was $2400.00

He sent a letter advising the producer to cease and desist running the footage and was told "So sue me" by the man that he had trusted with his dream. He now knows that his beloved daughter Amy, will undoubtedly watch his work on some television channel and receive no compensation. He believes that he was cheated out of a fortune and his talent mis-used during this experience.

He returned to East Tennessee determined to turn his latest lemon into sweet lemonade. He continued to perform and, much wiser now, picked up a few sponsors on his own. He attended the "Shot Show" in Dallas, Texas as the guest of ESPN. They had nothing to do with the swindle and he would love to appear on their network again. While in Dallas he met many people in the outdoor sports industry and continues to have a business relationship with some of them today. The Times-Mirror Company through their subsidiary "Field and

Stream Magazine" sold him a new Ford Van for $1.00 and Birchwood-Casey, Daisy, and Leupold-Stevens are current sponsors.

As had always been the case, he was doing well but had no promoter. He was learning, however and knew that a good agent would have protected him in his involvement with the producer for "American Shooter". He had been duped by every agent/promoter that he had become entangled with, so far at least, but continued to believe that the right one was still out there somewhere. He just wanted to entertain people with his amazing "gift" and let someone else handle the business. He had more disappointment to endure!

"You must meet with Triumph and Disaster and treat those two imposters just the same."

---Rudyard Kipling

World's Greatest Sharpshooter

Michael   Dana   Amy

Amy, 5 years old.
Already a proficient shooter.

Roger Webb.
Michaels Assistant.

CHAPTER TEN
"The Dream Reawakened"

The "World's Greatest Sharpshooter", reeling from the television experience, continued his career. He performed at several of the "Claybird Classic" events which were sponsored by Jeep. He was well paid for those exhibitions and enjoyed doing them. He had, in conjunction with The Daisy Manufacturing Company, begun a series of shooting safety seminars for children. He produced a shooting safety video which covers safety tips which are outlined in the Daisy manual. The seminars are now conducted at approximately ninety percent of his bookings and include a drawing for a Daisy Red Ryder BB Gun. They are very well received and he loves to do them. He compares children around guns in the same light as children around swimming pools. "You may not own a swimming pool but your children should know how to be safe around one" is the admonition that he has given to parents all across the country. Michael Blackburn does not advocate gun ownership but gun safety. He believes that a firearm is merely an object, a tool for hunting and self-defense, and in the proper hands, is totally safe. "A gun has never harmed anyone- It's people who do the harm", is a statement often heard at his performances. Safety is his primary concern and he has never had an accident during a performance in the many years that he has been an exhibition shooter.

Through his friend Russ Jette at Addieville East, a large shooting preserve in Rhode Island, he was asked to perform for a group of visiting Chinese dignitaries. The event had been arranged by the State Department and the shooter was glad to do it. This show created some lasting memories and the dignitaries seemed to love his show. The General in charge of the Chinese Army was in attendance and autographed one of the guns used in the exhibition. At the conclusion of the performance Michael related to the audience, "Oh by the way, everybody in the USA can shoot like this!"

Michael Blackburn's career is soaring again with several projects on the horizon. The shooter may very well be headed for television again. Michael Blackburn is one of a kind, he stands alone in this modern age. His track record when it comes to television speaks for itself. What he can bring to television has value, it merits the respect of all involved, from producers to the networks themselves. There are other shooters, even a few exhibition shooters, but there is only one Michael Blackburn. He is the greatest exhibition sharpshooter of all time.

The coming year will see "The Long Shot" become a reality. Using a special custom built 50 caliber rifle, Michael will break the long distance record. A six inch target will be used and the shot will be accomplished at a distance of over one mile. The rifle, built by Bud Burkey from Grey,

Tennessee, uses the barrel from an F-15 fighter plane.

Bookings are coming in from all over the US and two are confirmed for Canada. With his big heart and his love for children still intact, Michael recently traveled to Lexington, Kentucky where he entertained patients at of the Shriner's Hospital. A deal has just been completed to make the "Old Mill", an East Tennessee landmark, the official Home of Michael Blackburn. A small area will be set aside for the display of some of Michael's memorabilia and he will be available at certain times to meet fans and autograph his book.

The shooter's loyalty to sponsors is legendary. His sponsor base will be re-evaluated, however, in the coming months. Information on how to book "The World's Greatest Sharpshooter" may be found at the end of this text.

World's Greatest Sharpshooter

Michael's van decorated by Field & Stream.

Field & Stream, RST Ltd., Birchwood Casey,
Ithaca Gun, Daisy — some of Michael's sponsors.

Michael's guns by Winchester

CHAPTER ELEVEN

Sponsors

Sponsors play an integral role in the success of many endeavors. The career of Michael Blackburn is no exception. A sponsor relationship must be beneficial to both parties in order to be successful and withstand the test of time. Sponsoring companies supply funds that are needed to escalate the image and success of a performer such as Blackburn. They also provide equipment such as guns, ammunition, targets, scopes, etc. which are an absolute necessity to a career such as Michael's.

Michael Blackburn, in turn, brings their products and or services to the forefront at every opportunity. He uses their products and gives samples to members of his audience. The positive association with "The World's Greatest" is also very powerful. People want to use products that they see famous people use, whether it be hair spray or automobiles. Michael has always insisted on using the best products in his performances and, in one case, must buy that product himself. The rifle ammunition that he has used for several years is a product that he considers to be the best on the market and he buys it. He will shoot approximately 100,000 rounds annually and has never had a mis-fire with this particular brand. At his shows, he refers to it as "Brand X." An agreement is being sought at this time with the maker of this superior product.

The outdoor sports industry is a large and varied field serving a multitude of sports enthusiasts. They have a wide range from which to enlist the service of a spokesperson. There are race car drivers, olympic stars (including shooters), world class hunters, football stars, and the list goes on and on. There are a few exhibition shooters in the world today and most of them are very good at what they do such as fast draw pistol shooting. The fact remains, however, that there is only one Michael Blackburn, and he has the unchallenged title of "World's Greatest." No person on the sport shooting scene today has the potential to carry a sponsor's positive message as far with such integrity and talent.

Here's the story of Michael's associations with various sponsors along the way. They are not listed in any particular order but have all played an important part in his career.

Birchwood-Casey

The shooter had met some of the folks from this company at the "Shot Show" in Dallas, Texas and had used their gun care products for years. It was, however, during a performance at the "Jeep Claybird Classic" in Minnesota that he was approached by the company's advertising firm about a possible sponsor relationship. He was asked to give away some of their products during that performance. Of course, he gladly agreed. It was the beginning of a long and good relationship. Michael considers their gun care products to be the best on the market and continues to distribute samples for them at each of his shows.

Mike Wenner and Shawn Nahan, with the company's gun care products division now handle the relationship and are great gentlemen to work with. They have been instrumental in the production of this book and have been chosen, by Michael as the "Sponsor of the Year" for 1997.

Times-Mirror

A corporate giant and owner of "Field and Stream Magazine", they sponsored "The American Shooter" show from the beginning. After the first year, while at the "Shot Show", they invited Michael to a corporate party in Dallas. It was a grand event and was attended by executives from many sports related companies. Leupold, Birchwood-Casey, Jeep, Daisy, Colt were some of the companies represented. Michael's relationship with some of his sponsors today began at this party. He met Bob Hanna that night, a man that he grew to admire and who he would meet again. During a "Jeep Claybird Classic" shooting match held at Cherokee Rose Shooting Range in Georgia, Hanna told the shooter that he was working on a deal to give him a new Ford van. The van had been given to Field and Stream by the Ford Motor Company and had been customized with all the latest outdoor sporting equipment. It had been featured in an article by Field and Stream and had been built as the "Ultimate Sportsman's Vehicle". Bob Hanna told the shooter that a lawyer was drawing up the paperwork on the deal and that he would be contacted when everything was ready.

Bob finally called and said "Come to Two Park Avenue in New York City, the van is yours." "New York City" the shooter thought to himself, "I've never done a show there." Michael flew up to the "Big Apple" and was met at the airport by Bob Hanna. He asked the country boy if he had ever been on a subway. He received a look of utter disbelief as an answer. The two men rode the subway to lunch at a seafood restaurant somewhere in New York City. The shooter saw a new world that day - an underground world. Michael remembers vividly that the soup had cost $27.00 a bowl.

They proceeded to the office where Michael gave the executive $1.00 in exchange for the keys and title to the van. The $1.00 had made the transfer legal and binding. At this point Michael was told about all the high tech options that had been added to the van, especially the alarm system. The van was well protected from break-in or theft since it had a built-in gun cabinet and was designed with the sportsman in mind. Michael, in his excitement didn't hear too much of the explanation, he was more concerned about how he was going to get out of New York City.

Seeing the shooter's worry, Bob Hanna agreed to drive for a short distance since it would be on his way home anyway. The two men got in the van, with Bob driving, and started the trip. After a short distance, they stopped at a traffic light and Hanna told the shooter; "Here's where I get out, just follow this street and go through the Holland tunnel where you'll see signs for the Interstate." Michael climbed over the console and into the driver's seat and, with Hanna now out of sight and the light turning green, the engine died. The country boy from East Tennessee had never seen so much traffic in his life. Horns were honking and people were yelling. One guy yelled, "Why don't you get a new van", and the shooter replied; "This is a new van but I only paid a dollar for it." He had created a huge traffic jam and feared being shot or stabbed because of it. He started pushing buttons, the van had plenty of them, and the vehicle finally started. Now on the move, it seemed as though there were a million cars behind him as he entered the Holland tunnel where the van died again. Another van, directly behind the shooter, began to run into the rear of the new vehicle and, afraid for his life, he just put it into neutral. He was pushed through the tunnel, through a red light, and into a parking lot. He got out to survey the damage and to his amazement there was no damage to his vehicle. The other van, however, was another story, it had suffered extensive damage to the front end. Michael was apologizing for having caused the traffic jam when he realized that the man could not speak English. The other man, frustrated from the experience, simply drove away.

The shooter started pushing buttons again and finally got the vehicle to start. He drove out of the city and stopped at the first rest stop to calm down. He had just experienced traffic in New York City and his nerves were shot. He stayed the night in the van and got an early start for home the next morning. The van continued to die all the way home due, he later discovered, to the high tech alarm system. He had been inadvertently pushing a floor mounted button which was

71

designed to kill the engine should he be car-jacked. "It's funny now but it wasn't then", says Michael today. "I took the alarm system out and installed a 12 gauge shotgun and I haven't had any trouble since" he relates. The agreement required Michael to maintain insurance coverage and to display the Field and Stream logo on the van for a period of three years. The contract has expired and several calls to the giant company have failed to turn up a single person who knows that he van was given to Michael. Another magazine sponsor is being sought at this time.

Colt

Michael was invited to attend a meeting with some Colt executives while in Dallas so he decided to go. The CEO joked with the shooter about having so much hair and asked what kind of handguns he wanted. "Single action armies", was the reply and the company provided a beautiful matching set. Michael loved those pistols and shot them during many performances. Sadly, he was threatened by an agent who wanted them for himself. He turned them into a sheriff's department in North Carolina for return to Colt. He later learned that the promoter ended up with them after all. Colt is a great American company which is steeped in history and they make a fine product. Michael was proud to wear those two gold plated colts and would be proud to do so again. As of this writing the company has refused to renew the relationship.

World's Greatest Sharpshooter

Ithaca Gun

Ithaca is an old line company and is also steeped in tradition. They are current sponsors and have supplied Michael with 12 gauge shotguns. The bottom ejection system on these guns have resulted in a real crowd pleaser during Michael's performances. The empty shell casings are thrown high into the air and in rapid succession are hit with the next load. Michael is working on a shot called the "21 gun salute" where he will shoot 21 shell casings in a row using three Ithaca shotguns. He can also accomplish the same feat using the rifled "Deerslayer" barrels.

Ithaca shotguns are well made, by hand in Kings Ferry, New York. Michael tells his audiences, "If they were good enough for Annie, they're good enough for me."

Leupold Rifle Scopes

Leupold was a sponsor of "The American Shooter" segments during Michael's tenure on ESPN. He had never before used scopes but has now developed some amazing shots using Leupold's product. Michael has performed for the company's staff and has toured their plant in Beaverton, Oregon. Mike Slack, the company's owner is interested in shooting sports and collects old west memorabilia. The relationship has been a good one.

Daisy

Working closely with John Ford, a Daisy executive, Michael put together shooting safety seminars for children.

These have been very well received by kids as well as parents. At a recent show the entire county school system bussed the students to Michael's seminar. He believes that if only one accident is prevented, then the effort will have been worthwhile. These safety sessions with children are Michael Blackburn's first love. Daisy provides some of the bb guns that are given away at these seminars.

RC Sports Unlimited

This great company, owned by the Russ Jetty Family in Rhode Island, provides the shotgun shells that Michael uses in all his performances. These shells are manufactured in New Hampshire by a company named RST. Michael Blackburn believes them to be the best target loads in the industry. They are "Made by shooters for Shooters" and are a very exclusive product. They are not available everywhere but may be ordered by writing:

RC Sports Unlimited, Inc.
P.O. Box 401
Pascoag, RI 02859

There have been other companies that have supplied products and services to Michael. They are:

Barret Arms Company, Bridgestone/Firestone Tires, Carroll Bullets, Dixie Gunworks, Hamilton Dry Goods, and Wilson Case Company.

74

CHAPTER TWELVE

People who have made a Difference

It has been said that no person is an island. Most of us, at one time on another, have had to rely on other people during the course of our lives. Michael Blackburn is no exception. And so, he has many people to thank for his success. There is, of course, a danger involved when one begins to publicly say "Thank You." Even though making every effort to not do so, it is possible to leave someone out. This possibility could easily be avoided by making a general statement of appreciation to everyone. However, Michael feels so strongly about many of the relationships he holds so dear that he is willing to take the risk. He views this book as the proper vehicle to render many well deserved and heart felt thank you's. Michael feels that if anyone has been overlooked, it was not intentional, but simply an oversight. Everyone who has had an impact on Michael's career and life cannot be mentioned here but his intent is to recognize the major contributors.

Michael's family has played the most important roles in shaping him into the individual that he has become by simply believing in him when no one else would. It has been said that success requires "stickability" and is 90 percent "stick" and only 10 percent ability. Michael Blackburn has "stickability" and so many of his friends when it concerns his career. They have continued to believe in him through the ups and downs and have stayed with him no matter what happened. His wife, Dana and daughter Amy have lived through the downside of his career and have never wavered in their support. His parents Bob and Pat Blackburn gave him life and molded him into the sensitive and caring person that he is today. It is also possible that they, through some miracles of genes, gave him his remarkable vision and his brother, Pat has helped him in several performances.

Here are listed some others, in no particular order, that have impacted "The World's Greatest Sharpshooter" in a positive way.

Bob Hanna
The executive with Field and Stream magazine who worked the deal for the Ford van which is now called "The Freedom Express."

Bud Burkey
Michael's personal gunsmith. He built the special .50 caliber rifle and will serve as the ballistics expert for the "The Long

Shot."

Tom and Mildred Donly
They have never stopped believing in Michael and have lent financial support and valuable advice.

Glen Donly
The son of Tom and Mildred and a true friend. He has served as an assistant in many shows and has been supportive through thick and thin.

The City of Salem, Illinois
Michael's home town of which he is extremley proud. They erected a sign exclaiming the fact that he was the "World's Greatest Sharpshooter" for the whole world to see. They respected his talent.

William Lee and Brenda Golden
The singer for the "Oak Ridge Boys" and his lovely wife have given inspiration and friendship when it was needed most.

James Bequette
An executive of "Shooting Times" magazine and an avid supporter.

Steve Hill
A promoter from Abington, Virginia who has booked Michael to entertain at his events over the course of several years. An ex executive for a major television network, Steve will be involved in marketing the serires, "Shots that Won the West."

Mike Wenner

An executive in the gun care products division of Birchwood-Casey. He was the moving force in setting up what has become a wonderful sponsorship arrangement.

Shawn Nahan

Shawn handles the day-today workings of the arrangement with Birchwood-Casey and is an asset to that firm.

Lloyd Dougherty

The owner of the "Dixie Angler" Radio Network and a true believer. He has been there for the shooter with financial help and good advice.

Charlie Rhodes

Now with Guns and Ammo Magazine, Charlie was instrumental in the relationship with U.S. Repeating Arms, Co. (Winchester).

Annie Oakley

Though long gone, the spirit and accomplishments of this legendary shooter have given Michael much inspiration. Even though a recent discovery revealed that she had used shot shells in her .22 rifles, Michael still feels a sadness about breaking her records.

Roger Webb

A close friend and assistant at many shows. He has become like a brother to Michael.

George Mallard and Joe Hupp

These two Nashville promoters, while unable to help, were honest and forthright with the shooter. They played a very important role in that, because of them, the young shooter kept the faith that there really were honest promoters out there somewhere.

Mike Slack

The owner of Leupold-Stevens. The two share a love for the history of the old west.

Russ, Cindy and Charis Jettee

A family of friends in Rhode Island. Russ, a world class shooter himself, was instrumental in arranging Michael's performance for the Chinese dignitaries at Addieville East Farm. The Jette's are among the shooter's closest and most loyal friends.

Chris Phoenix

A gunsmith and friend in Illinois who was an early believer in Michael's talents and abilities.

There have been hundreds of show promoters and event coordinators who have booked Michael Blackburn to perform at their events. Bookings are the "life blood" of an entertainer's career and there have been many. Thanks to all of you who have scheduled Michael to perform throughout his twenty year career.

The biggest thanks must be directed to the fans who have attended performances in all kinds of weather and written so many wonderful letters over the years. Michael's loyalty to his fans is well known and he will remain on location as long as it takes to sign autographs for anyone who desires one. He recently stood in ankle deep mud to talk to fans and sign autographs. He does these things because he realizes that, without fans, there would be no reason to continue.

CHAPTER THIRTEEN

"How to Hit The Target"

Although having no formal training, Michael Blackburn has been hitting his targets for well over thirty years. He served a one year stint as a shooting instructor for the F.B.I. in Illinois and is a prodigy in marksmanship. Over the years, he has given one-on-one training to many people.

His desire is to help others develop a heartfelt respect for firearms and safety. He does not advocate gun ownership. Rather, he advocates gun safety. He knows that the gun is wrapped up in the history of this country and the freedom that we all enjoy. He wants to entertain his audiences while keeping a tradition alive! He would like to be remembered simply as a "Straight Shooter!"

Here are some tips from the "World's Greatest Sharpshooter."

1. Shooting begins with properly placed feet. They should be placed apart at least the breadth of the shooters shoulders but the position should be comfortable and relaxed.

2. The legs must not be locked but slightly bent so as to have a springing action. The lead foot should point directly toward the direction of the shot or slightly to the right or left depending on the shooter's orientation. (Right or left handed.)

3. Learn to control your breathing and to relax. You should take 3 or 4 long and deep breaths before each shot. The shot should be taken just after exhaling the last breath. Improper control of breathing will cause the shooter to pull off the target.

4. Do not grip the gun too tightly but in a relaxed manner. The butt of the stock on a long gun should be held tightly against the muscle of the shoulder.

5. Concerning focus, Michael's great gift, you must learn to keep both eyes open while looking down the barrel. Start with the rear sight, then the front sight. When you focus on the target one of the sights may become out of focus. This is

normal if you are properly focused on the target since absolute focus can be accomplished on only one distance at a time. Now place the out-of-focus sight on the target and fire.

6.   Aerial shots are performed using the same focusing techniques but another element must be added. You must believe that the target will be hit. Attitude is vital to hitting aerial targets much the same as putting a basketball through the hoop. Michael states that "I am strong on attitude. There have been occasions that I have heard shooters making excuses about why there were going to miss a target before they ever took their guns out of the holsters or cases. With that attitude, their shooting won't improve. You must believe in your ability to hit the target."

7. Misses are important because every shooter can learn from them. Everyone, no matter how skilled, will miss from time to time. Michael's comments on this subject are; "Misses are very important to me and I take credit for them all. When I miss I have the opportunity to learn what I did improperly and correct it. I am never satisfied with my shooting and always want to do better. I have done many shows without a single miss but am never satisfied. In some cases a hit might have been luck instead of marksmanship. Luck is not what I'm looking for."

8.   When shooting aerial targets remember to "come up" behind the target. Imagine that your target has a vapor trail, like a comet, and move up the tail with a steady swinging motion. You should see through the target and follow through after the shot much like a batter hitting a baseball.

9. Perfect shooting is attained by perfect practice. Practice consistently and learn from your misses. You will soon learn that the "perfect shot" cannot be heard by the shooter and ammo must be stored in a separate location in a locked container.

Michael did most of his learning by shooting a Daisy Red Ryder bb gun and it is a fine tool for the beginner. You should start with paper targets and will soon learn where the gun is shooting. You can then "sight in" your Daisy by shooting three round groups. If two out of three shots are closely grouped and you accomplish three such groups then you know where the gun is shooting. You have it "sighted in." Now you can concentrate on the misses in the groups to determine what you are doing wrong.

Remember when adjusting your sights to move the rear sight. If the gun is shooting to the left move the sight to the right. If you are shooting low you must raise the rear sight. Always move the rear sight in the direction that you want the bullets to go.

10. Concentrate on the amount of finger that you have on the trigger. Too little or two much will pull the gun off the target. Since this varies with each shooter you will have to discover the amount of finger that is best for you. Michael actually marks his finger with an ink pen and places that mark on the trigger for every shot.

"I hope that these tips will encourage all of you to be better marksmen and, above all, better citizens and neighbors."
---Michael Blackburn

EPILOGUE

And so, what of this man who is called "The World's Greatest Sharpshooter?" Is he special, different from other shooters? How could he possibly survive all the trials and tribulations sketched in this book and "keep on keepin on?"

He goes on, somehow, taking with him the most awesome shooting talent that mankind has ever seen. He is on a mission to teach gun safety to anyone, especially children, who will listen. He has been down but never out, he has walked through the valley but has seen the mountain top , he will never quit. A new day has dawned in Michael's career, he is in good hands. All that is required of him now is to take his show to the people who love him, his fans. He is still young and the future is bright.

He is living proof that history does indeed repeat itself, a throwback to the days of the old west. He would have fit right in a hundred years ago when "Buffalo Bill" Cody was touring the world with his famous troupe of sharpshooters. He has duplicated and surpassed every documented shot performed by the legends of yesteryear, including his favorite, "Little Sure Shot" - Annie Oakley. His prowess does not include "trick" shooting, it is all real, many times unbelievable, but real nontheless. What you see is what you get with both man and his shooting. He possesses a God given talent that is absolutely amazing.

He rountinely, during outdoor performances, turns a powerful Ithaca 12 gauge shotgun into an instrument of grace and perfection. The roar of each rapid shot and the casings going into oblivion seem to be a symphony in slow motion. His witty humor and laid back country ways, coupled with the admonition "You can be anything that you want to be" make his performances something to be remembered. He is the consummate professional and will perform in any weather.

His career is now soaring with bookings coming in from all across the country. A pilot for a series "Shots that Won the West" will be filmed soon and the record breaking "Long Shot" is fast approaching the front burner. The Old Mill, in Pigeon Forge, Tennessee, has set aside space for a small museum to display memorabilia. He will be there, in person, when he's not on the road to meet folks and autograph this book. It is a place with a rich heritage and is fitting to be called "The Home of Michael Blackburn". The owners of the Old Mill, Ben Frizzell and Al Blanton are to be commended for showing such respect for a living legend. You may be interested in booking Michael at an event, and if so, you should contact:

Arrowhead Classics Publishers
126 Connely Street, Suite 1
Sevierville, TN 37862
(423) 429-0252

Could it really be possible for one man to possess such a talent? Even though it sounds unbelievable, it is true. Keep your eyes on the night sky, there is a star that is getting brighter and brighter!

LEUPOLD®

Made Right. Made Here.

LEUPOLD & STEVENS

In this, our 90th year, Leupold & Stevens, Inc. is proud to note that Leupold products are symbols of all that is good about our sport. We're equally proud that our customers are possessive about the brand. So to honor them, our history is retold here, including the incident that led to our first hunting scope.

Like many American traditions, we have European roots. Sixteen-year-old Markus Friederick "Fred" Leupold immigrated from Germany to Boston in 1901 as a precision machinist. In 1907, he established a repair business for surveying equipment. By 1911, the firm had begun manufacturing surveying equipment. J. C. Stevens became a partner in 1914. Stevens had invented an unprecedented device to record the flow of water. So the company set out to capitalize on the invention. At the same time Fred Leupold's eldest son, Marcus, joined the firm. In 1930, Marcus was hunting the west side of Oregon's Cascade Range. A nice Blacktail buck presented itself, and Marcus fired. He missed because the scope he was using fogged internally. Worse still, the scope was difficult to adjust with any precision. Marcus and Bob set out to build a better scope. The result of this effort was the "Plainsman" - the first Leupold riflescope. The most water-resistant scope of its era, it featured internal adjustments, which meant that the maintube of the scope was permanently sealed. By 1960, just 13 years after the introduction of the Plainsman, Leupold scopes were becoming one of the markets premier brands.

TO LOCATE DEALERS NEAR YOU, CALL 1-800-929-4949

Celebrating a 50 Year Tradition

When Walter Mason set out in the 1940's to create a cold process gun blue for home use, he was trying to avoid paying $50 and waiting six weeks for a factory blueing of his own guns. Little did he realize that this effort would lead to creation of two chemical companies which later would merge to become BIRCHWOOD CASEY.

Walter Mason had been a chemistry major at Notre Dame but his education was interrupted by WWII. During post-war years he worked successfully at a variety of jobs, but his yearning for chemistry continued so strongly that finally he set up a lab in his basement to devote to full time to his first love. The liquid gun blue which led to the founding of Birchwood Chemical Company came out of this laboratory.

Mason wanted no part of a day-to-day company management. His love was the lab, and product after product took shape there. Casey Chemical Company was founded to handle some of these ideas, and some products from the Birchwood line were duplicated to merchandise under the Casey label.

Celebrating a 50 Year Tradition

Mason died in 1959, and his two companies were acquired and merged by a new management group in 1965. Two of the new owners were founders of Fuller Laboratories, Inc., and veterans of the pharmaceutical industry. With this background, they added further emphasis on science to the legacy of product originality and reliability which Mason had established.

For three years, BIRCHWOOD CASEY was operated as an independent company, but its orbit drew ever closer to its kissin' cousin, Fuller Laboratories. It was inevitable that the two should merge, and they did in August, 1968, with BIRCHWOOD CASEY becoming an autonomous division within Fuller Laboratories. In 1979 BIRCHWOOD CASEY was incorporated as BIRCHWOOD LABORATORIES, INC.

The BIRCHWOOD CASEY research and development function today is far more diversified and intensive than ever before. New ideas evolve constantly through laboratory and field testing-keeping the hunter, collector and hobbyist excited about enhancing, preserving, and using firearms.

Birchwood Laboratories, Inc.
7900 Fuller Road □ Eden Prairie, MN 55344
1-800-328-6156
Call for our free catalog and Gun Cleaning Tips!

The Old Mill - Pigeon Forge, Tennessee

Step back in time to relive a bygone era at our famous Old Mill, built in 1830. The mill is listed on the national register of historic places, and is one of the most photographed mills in the country. Take a guided tour and see how our water powered gristmill grinds corn, wheat, rye, and buckwheat daily using the same machinery that was considered antique a hundred years ago. Visit our general store where you can purchase these stone ground mill products, as well as other merchandise including crafted gift items, locally made jams and jellies, country ham, and our own homemade fudge made next door at our restaurant. Come experience this very special place where time stands still and memories are made to last forever.

The Old Mill Restaurant

Enjoy the kind of home cooked meal that made southern cooking famous. Try our mouth watering fried chicken or our great tasting country ham. You'll love our southern fried catfish or our homemade chicken and dumplings. All dinner specialities are served with our signature corn chowder, fritters, salad, fresh vegtables and free dessert! Many products made at the mill are used in recipes at our restaurant. You'll think there's a taste straight from Grandma's kitchen in every bite! We are open daily for breakfast, lunch, and dinner.

Phone (423) 453-4628 □ Web site: www.old-mill.com.